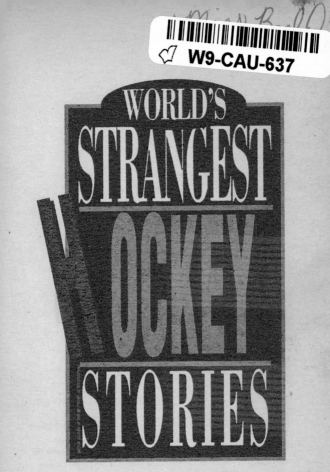

WORLD'S
STRANGEST
HOCKEY
STORIES

by Bart Rockwell

Watermill Press

Cover illustration by Paulette Bogan.

LIBRARY OF CONGRESS CATALOGING-IN-PUBLICATION DATA
Rockwell, Bart, (date)
   World's strangest hockey stories / by Bart Rockwell.
      p.   cm.
   Summary: Brief anecdotes of funny and bizarre happenings during a
century of hockey.
   ISBN 0-8167-2936-0 (lib. bdg.)   ISBN 0-8167-2853-4 (pbk.)
   1. Hockey—United States—Anecdotes—Juvenile literature.
2. Hockey—Canada—Anecdotes—Juvenile literature.   3. National
Hockey League—Anecdotes—Juvenile literature.   [1. Hockey—
Anecdotes.]   I. Title.
GV847.25.R63   1993
796.962'0973—dc20
                                                    92-25992

FLOWER POWER

In 1906 the old Montreal Wanderers won the Stanley Cup trophy. The Wanderers were so thrilled over their victory that the team went to a photography studio to be photographed with their trophy. After the pictures were taken, the team hurriedly left to celebrate their big win. Unfortunately, the Wanderers forgot to take their trophy with them. They left the Stanley Cup at the photography studio and forgot all about it. The Cup stayed at the studio until it was found by the photographer's elderly mother, who decided to use it as a flowerpot!

Much later the Montreal Wanderers' officials finally realized that its prize trophy was missing. Frantically, the team officials went hunting for it. They finally found hockey's greatest trophy stuffed with flowers in the photography studio. The team reclaimed its prize, and the Stanley Cup was saved from being used as a flowerpot for the rest of its days.

THANKS, PAL

The Philadelphia Flyers and the Minnesota North Stars were deadlocked at one goal each in the first round of a 1980 Stanley Cup playoff game when a strange thing happened. Minnesota was swarming the Philadelphia end of the rink looking to score the go-ahead goal when the Flyers' Bill Barber stole the puck. Barber escaped his own end and fired a wild slap shot at the Minnesota net, where Gary Edwards was tending goal. Edwards easily blocked the shot as Philadelphia players stormed in on him. The puck ended up on the stick of the North Stars' defenseman Brad Maxwell. Maxwell had to get rid of the puck in a hurry. He took a wild swing at it and sent it skidding back toward his own goalie, Gary Edwards. The puck hit Edwards' skate and trickled into his own net for a Flyers' goal! Bill Barber got credit for the goal because he was the last Philadelphia player to touch the puck. However, the truth was that Minnesota shot the puck into its own net to give the Flyers a 2–1 lead. With a little help from the unlucky North Stars' defenseman, Philadelphia went on to win the contest.

WHY CAN'T WE GET ALONG?

Jim Dorey of the Toronto Maple Leafs was called for *nine* penalties in a game against the Pittsburgh Penguins on October 16, 1968. He was assessed with a total of 48 penalty minutes!

OUCH!

When an Australian team took on a team from New Zealand on March 15, 1987, in a world championship ice hockey game, the result was a painful one for New Zealand. Australia beat New Zealand 58–0 to set a record for the most lopsided hockey win in world championship history.

THINK QUICK

Doug Smail of the Winnipeg Jets set an NHL record in a game against the St. Louis Blues on December 20, 1981, when he scored a goal just five seconds after the opening whistle. Bryan Trottier of the New York Islanders equaled that five-second scoring record in a game against the Boston Bruins on March 22, 1984.

Claude Provost of the Montreal Canadiens outdid both Smail and Trottier in an NHL game against the Boston Bruins on November 9, 1957. Provost scored a goal only *four* seconds after the start of a period of play, but his goal came at the beginning of the second period. Denis Savard of the Chicago Blackhawks (spelled Black Hawks prior to 1985–86 season) also scored a four-second goal, in the third period of a game against the Hartford Whalers played on January 12, 1986.

WHAT A STEAL

Professional hockey in Montreal was so popular during the 1956–57 season that some fans would do anything to get tickets to a Canadiens' home game. That season, a Montreal fan named Tom Donohue reported to police that thieves had broken into his home. The only thing the burglars had stolen was $385.00 worth of Canadiens season tickets!

POLICING THE ICE

Referees have always had a lot of critics. In 1895 two officials refereed a game between teams from Ottawa and Quebec. The game was played in Quebec and the home team was upset 3–2 by the visitors. After the officials left the arena, they were grabbed by angry Quebec fans who forced the officials back onto the rink, even though the game was over. The fans wanted the officials to declare the game a draw despite the score. The police had to be called in to rescue the anxious officials from the irate Quebec fans.

LONG NIGHT

When the Rochester Americans took on the New Haven Night Hawks in an American Hockey League (an NHL minor league) contest on April 11, 1982, everyone expected it to be a long game, but not as long as it actually turned out to be. When the two teams had met days earlier, it took two overtime periods to decide a game that had ended in a 7–7 tie at the conclusion of regulation play.

When the April 11th game ended with the score knotted at 2–2, the overtime periods began again. When the first overtime period ended, the score was still tied. After the second and third overtimes concluded, the teams were still deadlocked. Finally, in the fourth overtime period, Warren Holmes of the Night Hawks tallied a goal to give New Haven a 3–2 victory. The game lasted 6 hours, 14 minutes, and 8 seconds. The game had begun on Saturday night and hadn't ended until Sunday morning. To top things off, the goalies on both teams played the entire game without any substitutes.

HATS OFF

G len Harmon was a defenseman for the Montreal Canadiens in 1948–49. Glen's wife owned a hat shop in Montreal that was often visited by the wife of Butch Bouchard, the Montreal Canadiens' team captain. Mrs. Bouchard fell in love with an expensive hat, and so Glen Harmon delivered it to the Montreal Forum before a hockey game against the Detroit Red Wings. Harmon showed the hat to Butch Bouchard, who groaned when he learned how much it had cost. Being a good sport, Harmon offered to give Bouchard the hat free of charge if he scored two goals that night against Detroit. Harmon didn't feel that he was risking much because Bouchard had scored only four goals so far that season—and the season was already half over.

But Bouchard made his wife very happy that evening. He went out and scored two goals to give his team a 2–0 victory over Detroit. He also won a free hat!

OH, MY ACHING BACK!

G oaltender Glen Hall of the Chicago Black Hawks played an amazing 553 consecutive games in net (including regular season games and playoff games) before a strained ligament in his back caused him to finally miss a game during the 1962–63 season.

HAT TRICK

When a modern hockey player scores three or more goals in a single game, the feat is referred to as a "hat trick." To celebrate the accomplishment, some fans at professional hockey games toss old hats onto the ice.

Did you ever wonder where the term "hat trick" came from? It originally had nothing to do with ice hockey. The expression originated in the English game of cricket around 1882. It was used to describe the feat of a bowler taking three wickets on successive balls. As a reward for that accomplishment, the bowler was given a new hat by his cricket club.

Experts believe that the term was first used in connection with ice hockey in the early 1900's. At that time it was used to describe three successive goals scored by one player without any other goals being scored by either team in between.

Today, however, "hat trick" is used to describe three or more consecutive or nonconsecutive goals scored by a single player in a game. Fans continue to toss hats onto the ice to celebrate that great feat whenever it occurs. And the ritual all started at a cricket match.

DON'T CHICKEN OUT

The Los Angeles Kings had a poor NHL season in 1987–88, going 30–42–8 for the year. In a home game against the Montreal Canadiens, which the Kings went on to lose, one Los Angeles fan had an insulting way of showing his feelings about the Kings' performance. He sneaked a live chicken into the arena and dressed it in a tiny purple uniform (purple was the color of the Kings' uniforms at the time). During the game, he tossed the live "uniformed" chicken out onto the ice. The chicken slipped all over the ice until it was finally captured and removed from the rink. Everyone thought the chicken stunt was very funny except the Los Angeles Kings. They thought it was quite a fowl deed!

QUICK SHOT

M ark Messier and Dave Lumley of the Edmonton Oilers got off to a quick start in their game against the Los Angeles Kings on March 29, 1982. Messier and Lumley set an NHL record by scoring one goal each within the first 24 seconds of the contest. The scores were the fastest two goals ever scored by two players on the same team at the start of an NHL game.

UNIFORM MADNESS

T he Boston Bruins traveled to Chicago to play the Black Hawks on January 3, 1979.
Unfortunately, the start of the game had to be delayed some 1½ hours after the originally scheduled starting time.

The problem was that even though the Boston players were on hand and ready to play, they didn't have anything to wear out onto the ice. The Bruins' uniforms had accidentally been delivered to *San Francisco* instead of to Chicago! After Boston's uniforms were delivered to the right city, the game finally took place.

SICK SHOWING

The Stanley Cup playoffs have been the world championship of ice hockey since 1894. It is the dream of every hockey player to one day be on a team that wins the Stanley Cup. However, in 1919 there was no Stanley Cup winner—and it was all because of a terrible flu epidemic that swept across North America.

In 1919 the Seattle Metropolitans (who were the champions of the Pacific Coast Hockey League) took on the Montreal Canadiens (who were the champions of the National Hockey League) in the Stanley Cup finals. After five games in the series had been played, the score was Montreal two wins and Seattle two wins, with the other game ending in a tie.

Before the sixth and deciding game was played, the terrible flu struck. Several Montreal players became sick, including star player Joe Hall, who had to be hospitalized. The Stanley Cup's final game was postponed when Hall suddenly died from the disease. Health officials ordered the Stanley Cup playoffs cancelled. The series was never settled. It ended with the teams tied at two games apiece. It was the first and only time since 1894 that a Stanley Cup champion was not crowned.

HOT STUFF

The Montreal Wanderers, one of the original teams in the NHL when it was first formed in 1917, dropped out of the league in 1918 for a very good reason. Montreal's home ice rink burned down that year, and the Wanderers couldn't find a place to play their home games!

OH SAY! CAN YOU SEE?

T he Detroit Red Wings visited Boston to take on
the Bruins in an NHL game on November 10,
1948. Play started on time but after only nine
minutes the officials had to halt the action.
Conditions on the ice had made it just too dangerous
to continue. Everyone agreed to postpone the game
for the safety of the players and to reschedule the
contest for the following day. Unbelievably, the
problem was due to fog—*inside* Boston Garden.
Humid conditions inside the building had caused a
thick fog to rise from the ice. The pea-soup fog was
so dense that players could not see well enough to
skate around. So thanks to a weird fog *inside* a
building, an NHL game was temporarily called off.

GOAL FOR AN NHL GOALIE

The National Hockey League was formed in 1917. From 1917 until 1979 no goalie had ever recorded a goal in an NHL game (even though goalies had scored in other leagues before). It seemed highly unlikely that an NHL goalie would ever score a goal until the New York Islanders took on the Colorado Rockies (now the New Jersey Devils) on November 28, 1979.

Late in the contest the Rockies were losing, so the Colorado coach removed his goalie to put an additional attacker on the ice. After the Islanders goalie blocked a Colorado shot, the puck bounced back to Rockies' defenseman Rob Ramage. Ramage made a terrible backwards pass that didn't connect with anyone. The puck skidded down the ice toward the unmanned Colorado goal and slipped into the net for an Islanders' goal. Rob Ramage of the Rockies actually shot the puck, but since Billy Smith was the last Islander to actually touch the puck, he got credit for the goal. And since Smith was a goaltender, he became the first NHL goalie to officially score in an NHL game.

STUCK IN GOAL

Goalie Terry Sawchuk played a lot of games between the posts during his NHL career. Sawchuk appeared in 971 games and registered 103 career shutouts during his 21 years in the NHL. Now that's one durable goalie.

A BROOKLYN CHEER!

B elieve it or not, there used to be an NHL team in Brooklyn, New York. In 1941, an NHL team named the Americans became the Brooklyn Americans. They played only one season of pro hockey as the Brooklyn Americans before dropping out of the league in 1942.

DON'T BLINK!

T he scoring was fast and furious during a game between the Toronto Maple Leafs and the New York Americans on March 19, 1938. In the third period of action in that contest the two teams scored an amazing eight goals in just 4 minutes and 52 seconds. Toronto scored five of those lightning-fast goals while the Americans tallied three. The Maple Leafs ended up winning the game 8–5.

MAJOR DEBUT

There have been many great rookie goal scorers in the National Hockey League. Wayne Gretzky, Mike Bossy, and Gordie Howe are just a few of those outstanding rookie scorers. Howie Meeker of the Toronto Maple Leafs was a great rookie scoring sensation, but few of today's hockey fans remember him. In fact, Meeker was the first NHL hockey player to pull off a rookie scoring feat that has seldom been duplicated.

Everyone knows that scoring a "hat trick" or three goals in a single game is a great feat. It's even a greater feat when accomplished by a rookie playing in his first NHL season. On January 8, 1944, rookie Howie Meeker not only notched a hat trick but went two steps further. Playing in a game against the Chicago Black Hawks, Meeker fired the puck into the Chicago net *five* times. He was the first NHL rookie player to ever score five goals in one game, even though he is not remembered as one of the game's greatest scorers. Unfortunately, a broken leg prematurely ended Meeker's career.

A LOT ALIKE

Tiny Thompson and Alex Connell were both NHL goaltenders. Thompson played for the Detroit Red Wings as well as the Boston Bruins. Connell also played for the Detroit Red Wings as well as the Ottawa Senators and other teams. They both played for 12 years in the NHL. And even though Alex Connell played fewer games (417) than Tiny Thompson (553), they both finished their careers with exactly 81 total shutouts!

HE'S EVERYWHERE

When the Ottawa Senators took on the Edmonton Eskimos in a Stanley Cup playoff game during the 1922–23 season, King Clancy of Ottawa was a jack-of-all-trades on the ice. Clancy played every position for Ottawa during the course of the contest, including *both* defensive spots and *all* forward positions. He even played *goal* for a while when Clint Benedict, the team's regular goalie, was penalized and sent off the ice. Clancy's amazing performance wasn't a publicity stunt—he just filled in where he thought he was needed. With King Clancy's help, Ottawa won the game and the series to advance to the Stanley Cup finals.

HANDS OFF!

When it's time for a faceoff in hockey, the official quickly drops the puck between the sticks of two opposing players. However, before 1914, officials had to actually place the puck on the ice with their hands. That rule led to a lot of officials with sore fingers and broken hands! To save wear and tear on officials the faceoff rule was changed in 1914, allowing them to just drop the puck.

STANLEY CUP CIRCUS

S eeing your home team play in the Stanley Cup
finals is the dream of every die-hard hockey fan.
A team that makes it to the finals of the Stanley Cup
playoffs normally gets to skate on its home ice before its
hometown fans at least a few times before the series is
decided. But that was not the case in 1950 for the New
York Rangers. That year the Rangers and the Detroit
Red Wings squared off in the best-of-seven series for the
Stanley Cup trophy.

Unfortunately for the Rangers, the circus had been
booked to play at Madison Square Garden, the Rangers'
home arena, at the same time the Stanley Cup playoffs
were going on. The circus and the Stanley Cup playoffs
both couldn't be held at the Garden, so hockey had to go!

The Rangers could not play a single game of the
1949–50 Stanley Cup finals on their home ice. Forced to
select a neutral site, they played what were supposed to
be their home games at Toronto's Maple Leaf Gardens.
The Rangers played as well as they could without any
home-ice advantage, but eventually lost the Stanley Cup
to the Detroit Red Wings four games to three.

STREET SMART

In 1924 the Montreal Canadiens, coached by Leo Dandurand, won the Stanley Cup playoffs and with it Lord Stanley's Cup. After their series against the Calgary Tigers had ended, the happy Montreal team took along the Stanley Cup trophy in one of their cars and went off to celebrate. As luck would have it, the car the trophy was in got a flat tire. When the players got out to change the flat, they took the Cup out of the car. When the tire was fixed they drove off, leaving the Stanley Cup sitting on a deserted street corner! Luckily, they remembered the Cup later and returned to find it exactly where they'd left it.

EXHAUSTED

The Detroit Red Wings traveled to the Montreal Forum on March 24, 1936, to take on the Montreal Maroons in what was supposed to be an ordinary playoff contest. However, the game ended in a 0–0 tie, and the ordinary became the extraordinary as a marathon hockey match began.

The Red Wings and Maroons went on to play five full overtime periods and remained deadlocked at 0–0. Finally, in the sixth overtime period, Mud Bruneteau of Detroit sent the puck flying past Montreal goalie Lorne Chabot to win the game for Detroit and end the longest overtime game in NHL playoff history.

The contest, which had begun at 8:34 P.M., ended at 2:25 A.M. the following morning, March 25. The game itself lasted 5 hours, 51 minutes from opening faceoff to winning shot. In all there was 2 hours, 56 minutes, and 30 seconds of actual playing time. To top things off, Detroit's goalie Norm Smith stopped 92 Montreal shots during the contest to record the NHL's longest single shutout game.

THAT'S A PENALTY?

When an NHL player commits a foul and is sent to the penalty box, his team has to play short-handed. Being outnumbered by the opposition is supposed to work against the team guilty of the infraction, but it didn't happen that way on May 12, 1981, when the New York Islanders faced off against the Minnesota North Stars in the first game of the 1980–81 Stanley Cup finals. In the first period of play, the Islanders' Bob Bourne was whistled for spearing Minnesota's Brad Maxwell and was sent off to serve a five-minute major penalty. That was supposed to give Minnesota a big scoring opportunity, but as it turned out, it was the Islanders who got the advantage.

A little over three minutes after Bourne was sent off the ice, New York's Bryan Trottier took a pass and scored a shorthanded goal against the North Stars' goalie. A mere 47 seconds later, Trottier stole the puck again from a Minnesota defenseman and fed it to his teammate Anders Kallur. Kallur promptly whacked the puck into the North Stars' net for the Islanders' second shorthanded goal in less than fifty seconds!

The North Stars were so rattled that they never did manage to capitalize on Bourne's five-minute penalty. They also went on to lose the game 6–3.

MONEY CAN'T BUY SUCCESS

The Montreal Maroons won the Stanley Cup in 1925–26, but could not repeat their success over the next few seasons. In order to beef up their team, the Maroons' management went on a spending spree to sign top-notch players for the 1928–29 season. The Maroons decided to spend and spend big to show up their crosstown rivals, the Canadiens, and, if they were fortunate, to make it to the Stanley Cup finals once again.

The Maroons promptly went out and spent $22,500 to sign star Hooley Smith. They signed Dave Trottier for $15,000 and Reg Noble for $7,000. Jimmy Ward was signed for a salary and bonus of $17,000. That was a lot of money in 1928–29.

Unfortunately, the money didn't prove to be a good investment. The Maroons ended up finishing dead last in the NHL's Canadian Division in 1928–29. To make matters even worse, the team that won the Canadian Division that year was the Montreal Canadiens. Things got even worse after that. The Canadiens won the Stanley Cup in 1929–30 and 1930–31. The Maroons didn't win the Stanley Cup again until 1934–35.

CURSES ON YOU, BLACK HAWKS!

The Chicago Black Hawks were coached by Pete Muldoon for the 1926–27 NHL season, and they did fairly well. Although the team was defeated in the first round of the Stanley Cup playoffs that season, they had been serious contenders, and Pete Muldoon expected praise from Chicago's management. Instead, he was fired. The Black Hawks wanted to start fresh with a new coach in 1927–28, and they let Muldoon go.

Pete Muldoon was so angry over his dismissal that he put a "curse" on the team. Pete hexed the Black Hawks by saying that they would never win the NHL regular-season  title for having the best record in the NHL. Of course no one paid much attention to the Muldoon Curse at first. But five years passed and the Black Hawks did not win the NHL season title. Another ten years went by and still Chicago did not finish first. The Muldoon Curse was taking its toll. The Black Hawks did not win a single NHL regular-season title from 1927–28 until 1966–67, when the Muldoon Curse was finally broken. It took some 40 years to snap the hex.

Luckily for Chicago, Pete Muldoon had not mentioned the Stanley Cup in his curse. The Black Hawks did qualify for the Stanley Cup playoffs several times during the hex years, and actually won the Stanley Cup three times during that period (1933–34, 1937–38, and 1960–61).

THANKS FOR THE BARGAIN
AND GOOD-BYE

T he New York Rangers entered the National
Hockey League during the 1926–27 season.
The team was owned by John Hammond, and he
hired a young hockey man from Toronto named Conn
Smythe to build and run his team. Smythe proved to
be not only a wise choice but a person who could
persuade good players to sign at bargain-basement
prices. Smythe quickly went to work building up the
Rangers. He signed well-known goalie Lorne Chabot
and future Hall of Fame players Ching Johnson, Bill
Cook, and Frank Boucher. Smythe also added star
players Taffy Abel, Murray Murdoch, and Bun Cook
(Bill Cook's brother) to his roster, along with 24
others. Amazingly, Conn Smythe built a roster of
fabulous hockey talent in 1926–27 without spending
a lot of money. Smythe signed all 31 players for only
$32,000!

How did owner John Hammond reward Smythe
for his hard work? He fired him before the Rangers
ever played their first game and hired someone else to
run the team! Smythe was angry about his dismissal,
but he got even. He went to Toronto, where the old
Toronto St. Patricks of the NHL were for sale.
Smythe scraped up the money he needed to buy the
club and renamed the team the Maple Leafs. Six
years later Conn Smythe's Toronto Maple Leafs beat
the New York Rangers to win the Stanley Cup.

SWITCHEROO

Paul Stewart was an NHL referee during the
1991–92 season. Like all referees, Stewart
assessed penalties against players for rule infractions
and fighting.

Unlike most referees, however, Paul Stewart was
an NHL player before he turned to officiating.
Stewart played 21 NHL games with the Quebec
Nordiques in 1979–80. Strangely enough, during
Stewart's short playing career he was considered a
tough guy whose forte was fighting!

GOALS GALORE

To be a winning team in the NHL, you've got to
have some great goal scorers. In 1977–78 the
Boston Bruins had a lot of those. In fact, the Bruins
had players on their team who scored 20 or more
goals that season. They were Peter McNab (41
goals), Terry O'Reilly (29), Bob Schmautz and Stan
Jonathan (27), Rich Middleton and Jean Ratelle (25),
Wayne Cashman (24), Greg Sheppard (23), Brad Park
(22), and Don Marcotte and Bob Miller (20).
Unfortunately, even with all those big guns, Boston
lost to the Montreal Canadiens in the Stanley Cup
finals four games to two!

WHO'S NEXT?

The Detroit Red Wings and the Toronto Maple Leafs met in the early rounds of the Stanley Cup playoffs in 1939–40. Toronto won the first game and was leading 3–1 in the second game when a huge fight broke out with only one minute remaining in the contest. Toronto's Red Horner suddenly became the busiest man on the ice. First he got into a battle with Detroit's Jack Stewart and then fought Jimmy Orlando. After that Horner mixed it up with Detroit's Ebbie Goodfellow and then matched muscle with Alex Motter. Horner held his own in all of the fights until he finally met his match. A female Detroit fan scrambled down to the edge of the hockey rink, smacked Horner with her purse, and then started yanking his hair! Horner knew then that it was time to give up. He quickly retreated to the safety of the Toronto dressing room!

FAST BUT NOT FAST ENOUGH

Consider the case of poor Carl Liscombe of the Detroit Red Wings. In 1938 Liscombe scored *3 goals in just 1 minute, 52 seconds* against the Chicago Black Hawks. That's an average of 1 goal every 37 $1/3$ seconds, yet that wasn't good enough to last as an NHL record! The current record (3 goals scored in only *21 seconds*) was set on March 23, 1952, by Bill Mosienko of the Chicago Black Hawks in a game against the New York Rangers. Read the story on page 47 to find out how Mosienko accomplished his amazing feat.

OLD STORY

There have been many great hockey stars who have scored 50 goals in a single season. Maurice "Rocket" Richard scored 50 goals in a 50-game season for the Montreal Canadiens in 1945. Mike Bossy of the New York Islanders had several 50-goal seasons, his first one coming in 1978, when there were more than 50 games in a season. Bossy also later equaled Richard's feat of scoring 50 goals in only 50 games. In 1981 hockey great Wayne Gretzky scored 50 goals in the first *39 games* of the season and tallied 92 goals for the 1981–82 season.

What's interesting about these great scoring marks is that the players who achieved them were so young. Maurice Richard was 23 when he tallied his 50 goals in 50 games. Mike Bossy was only 21 when he had his first 50-goal season. Gretzky scored 55 goals for the Edmonton Oilers in 1980–81 at the tender age of 18! Unfortunately, age seems to slow down the output of many great hockey scorers.

But John Bucyk of the Boston Bruins was quite an exception. In 1971 Bucyk was an old man by hockey standards when he blazed his 50th goal of the season against the Detroit Red Wings. Bucyk notched his first 50-goal season that year at the age of 35!

GETTING INTO HOT WATER

Coach Lester Patrick cooked up a crazy way that he thought would keep his New York Rangers healthy during the 1929–30 season. Patrick ordered everyone on his team to drink a glass of hot water when they woke up every morning.

BROTHER ACT

In June 1992 Brian Sutter was named the head coach of the Boston Bruins. Sutter, who was 36 years old at the time, was appointed head coach of the Bruins on June 10, 1992.

A mere two days later Brian's younger brother, Darryl, followed in his brother's footsteps. On June 12, 1992, 33-year-old Darryl was appointed head coach of the Chicago Black Hawks! Darryl also became the youngest active head coach in the NHL at that time.

NUMBERS GAME

Phil Esposito and Ken Hodge were great players for the Boston Bruins for many seasons.

As members of the Bruins, Esposito wore number seven and Hodge wore number eight. Late in their careers, Esposito and Hodge were both traded to the New York Rangers at the same time. The former Bruins players wanted to keep the numbers they'd worn in Boston, but found that two New York players already wore numbers seven and eight. Rather than switch to new numbers, Esposito and Hodge simply "doubled" their original numbers. As members of the New York Rangers, Phil Esposito wore number 77 and Ken Hodge wore number 88.

STRANGE ROAD TO NHL

enter Garry Unger was 19 years old in 1967 and still eligible to play another season of junior hockey in Canada when a strange twist of fate landed him in the NHL. Before reporting to the training camp of a minor-league team associated with the Toronto Maple Leafs, Unger suffered a knee injury and was sent to Toronto for treatment. While in Toronto he was invited to scrimmage with the Maple Leafs and looked impressive. By a strange stroke of luck for Unger, Toronto's Frank Mahovlich suddenly had to be hospitalized for an injury. That left a spot open on the Maple Leafs' roster. Since Unger was in Toronto and had looked good in scrimmages, he became an instant NHL player. But even more impressively, Unger went on to play 914 consecutive games for Toronto, Detroit, St. Louis, and Atlanta between February 24, 1968, and December 21, 1979, a record that wasn't broken until the 1986–87 season.

BASEBALL TOO

veryone knows that Wayne Gretzky is one of hockey's greatest players. But did you know that he was also a good baseball player? In 1980, during hockey's off-season, the 19-year-old Gretzky played for the Brantford Red Sox of the Inter-County Major League, a semipro league in southern Ontario. Gretzky, who batted over .400 that year, attracted the interest of the Toronto Blue Jays baseball team. However, Wayne decided to stick with hockey, and NHL hockey fans are sure glad he did!

SCORE TIED

The Art Ross Trophy is awarded annually to the top point scorer in the NHL. In 1962 awarding the Art Ross Trophy was a real problem. At the end of that 70-game regular season, Bobby Hull of the Chicago Black Hawks and Andy Bathgate of the New York Rangers had both totaled 84 points. The issue was resolved when Hull was named the winner of the trophy because he had scored 50 goals that season while Bathgate had tallied only 28 goals.

The only other time (as of 1991) that the NHL scoring race ended in a tie was in 1980. Marcel Dionne of the Los Angeles Kings and Wayne Gretzky of the Edmonton Oilers each scored 137 points in an 80-game season. Dionne was awarded the Art Ross Trophy because he had fired 53 goals into the net that year while Gretzky had scored only 51.

NO SECURITY

Frederic McLaughlin, the owner of the Chicago Black Hawks, was a tough man to work for. Being the coach of McLaughlin's team certainly didn't provide much job security. McLaughlin changed coaches 14 times from 1926 to 1940!

NOT SO COOL McCOOL

Goalie Frank McCool won the Calder Memorial Trophy as the NHL's best rookie player in 1945 as a member of the Toronto Maple Leafs. Despite his last name, however, McCool wasn't the coolest customer when it came to handling pressure. In fact, McCool suffered from stomach ulcers. He used to drink milk between periods to soothe his troublesome stomach.

SMILE WHEN YOU SAY THAT

Because of the rough nature of hockey, many players have had their teeth knocked out and have had to wear dentures. Bob Plager, who played for the St. Louis Blues in the mid-1970's, liked to kid around with false teeth. During a 10-day road trip to the West Coast, he swiped teammate Larry Keenan's false teeth and mailed them home to St. Louis!

On another occasion Plager was given a game misconduct early in an NHL contest and sent to the St. Louis locker room. While waiting there, he went from locker to locker switching his teammates' dentures!

NOT A GHOST OF A CHANCE!

Gilles Gratton, who played for the St. Louis Blues and the New York Rangers in the 1970's, had some unusual beliefs about reincarnation. Gratton believed that he had lived before as a Spanish soldier in the 14th century and had died in battle of a sword wound in the abdomen. He believed that was why he often awoke from deep sleeps with stomach pains!

DRESSING UP AND DOWN

Goaltender Gary Smith, who played for eight different NHL teams from 1965 to 1980, was an outstanding shot blocker who had an odd habit. Whenever a period ended and the team went to the locker room to rest, Gary would take off every stitch of his equipment and then put it back on again just before it was time to return to the ice. Smith dressed and undressed between *every* period. Why did he do it? Gary Smith claimed that all that dressing and undressing kept him from getting too nervous!

BROKEN RECORD

Bobby Baun of the Toronto Maple Leafs refused to let anything interfere with his playing in the Stanley Cup finals. In 1964, Baun was a defenseman for Toronto in the series that pitted the Maple Leafs against the Detroit Red Wings.

Detroit was leading the series three games to two when Baun faced off against Detroit's Gordie Howe with the game tied. Attempting to win the faceoff, Baun heard a loud "crack" in his ankle as his right leg collapsed under him. He was carried into the locker room and stayed there until the third period ended, with the score tied 3–3. After taking a local anesthetic to dull the throbbing pain in his ankle, Baun returned to the ice to play in sudden-death overtime—despite protests from the Toronto officials. Amazingly, he scored the winning goal to even the series at three games apiece.

With the seventh and final game of the Stanley Cup finals on tap, Baun refused to have his ankle X-rayed until the series concluded. No matter how much anyone argued, he insisted on playing in the final game no matter what condition his leg was in.

Baun played in game seven and Toronto won the Stanley Cup. Only after the Cup was in Toronto's hands did he agree to have his ankle X-rayed. It was then discovered that Baun had scored the winning goal in game six and played all of game seven of the series with a fractured ankle.

WE GIVE UP

Coach Roger Neilson of the Vancouver Canucks wasn't happy with the officiating of a game between the Chicago Black Hawks and his team in late March 1982. Neilson thought that the officials were working against his team, so he decided to surrender. He grabbed a white towel near his bench and began to wave it in the air like a white flag. Several Canuck players liked what they saw and did the same thing. Many of the Vancouver fans thought the stunt was funny, but the president of the NHL didn't. He levied a fine against the Canucks and their coach.

I FORGOT

Star defenseman Larry Robinson of the Montreal Canadiens traveled to Hartford, Connecticut, with his team to take on the Hartford Whalers in December 1981. When the game was over, the Canadiens players changed in the locker room and left, but Larry Robinson left behind some important belongings. A building attendant found Robinson's diamond-studded Stanley Cup championship ring from the 1978–79 season and a watch given to Robinson for being in the Canada Cup competition hanging on a hook in the visitors' locker room. Robinson had been in such a rush to leave that he'd left behind his jewelry, which was valued at thousands of dollars. Luckily for Larry, the honest attendant saw to it that Robinson's forgotten finery was returned to him.

GOOD HANDS

Murray "Muzz" Patrick was a tough defenseman for the New York Rangers in the late 1930's and early 1940's. Patrick was someone who could handle himself if a fight broke out on the ice. Before signing with the Rangers, he was an amateur heavyweight boxing champion in Canada and almost became a professional boxer in the United States, but opted for a pro hockey career instead.

I SEE!

During the 1936–37 season a strange hockey first occurred in the NHL. A player named Russ Blinco (pronounced Blinko) became the first NHL player to wear eyeglasses during a game.

TRAVELING LIGHT

Butch Goring of the Los Angeles Kings wasn't much of a packer for road trips during his NHL career. In fact, Butch was known to sometimes take along only a toothbrush when he left to play games on the road.

GOALIE GOOF

A modern hockey team has more than one goalie ready to play, in case of an injury to or poor performance by the starting goalie. But that wasn't the case in the early days of the sport. Teams were allowed to have only one goalie dressed for each game. If he got hurt, the team had to scramble around to find a quick substitute, which wasn't always easy to do.

On April 7, 1928, the New York Rangers and the Montreal Maroons were playing the Stanley Cup finals in Montreal when Ranger goalie Lorne Chabot was injured. Chabot's injury was so bad that he had to be taken out of the game. That left New York without a goalie. The Rangers' coach and manager, Lester Patrick, quickly looked around to find a sub. Sitting in the stands was Alex Connell, a goalie for another NHL team, the Ottawa Senators. According to the rules, Patrick could use the other goalie as a sub (even though he was only there to watch the game) if the coach of the Maroons agreed to let him. Unfortunately for the Rangers, the Maroons' coach, Cecil Hart, refused.

Patrick was frantic. He needed a goalie and quick. Finally the 45-year-old manager/coach decided that the only thing to do was to play goalie *himself*. Patrick was a former NHL star, but he had been a defenseman. Nevertheless, he put on the pads and went in to play goal for the Rangers in the Stanley Cup!

Amazingly, Lester Patrick played well in his Stanley Cup debut as an NHL goalie. He gave up only a single goal, and the game was tied at the end of regulation play. Then, because it was a playoff game, the contest went into a sudden-death overtime period. Patrick stayed in goal and held the Maroons scoreless until Frank Boucher of the Rangers scored the game-winning goal for New York. The Rangers won the game thanks to the strange and phenomenal performance of their 45-year-old coach!

Inspired by Patrick's game, the Rangers went on to win the Stanley Cup with the help of their regular goalie, Lorne Chabot, who returned to action after that night.

HEAVY-METAL SHOOTER

Yvan Cournoyer was a great scorer during his NHL career with the Montreal Canadiens. However, Cournoyer wasn't born with a great ability to shoot the puck. It was a skill he had to develop. When Yvan prepared to leave the Junior Canadiens, a minor-league team, to join their parent club in the NHL, Cournoyer's coach told Yvan to go home and work on strengthening his shot. Cournoyer did just that. He went home to his father's machine shop and made some solid-steel hockey pucks out of scrap metal. The pucks weighed about two pounds each. Yvan spent months in his cellar shooting the heavy pucks against thick carpets hanging from the rafters. The heavy-metal shooting practice sometimes shook the foundation of the Cournoyer house, but Yvan developed a strong, deadly shot that he put to good use during his NHL career.

HONORABLE GOALIE

Some people think of pro hockey players as tough guys who are better at using their muscles than their heads. Of course, that's far from true. Just look at Myles J. Lane, who played goal for the Stanley Cup champion Boston Bruins in the late 1920's. Myles was a graduate of Harvard Law School and later became a New York State Supreme Court Justice when his hockey career ended.

FACE THE MUSIC

E very modern goalie wears a protective face mask. With pucks hit at such incredible speeds, a face mask is essential for a goalie's safety. But until the 1959–60 season, no one had ever seen a goaltender wear a protective mask in the NHL. The first NHL goalie to use a mask was Jacques Plante of the Montreal Canadiens.

In the 1959–60 season, Plante was a 31-year-old goalie who had won the Vezina Trophy as the league's best goaltender several times. Plante, who had suffered two fractured cheekbones earlier in the season, had taken to wearing a protective mask of his own design in practice, but not in games. Then on November 1, 1959, a shot by New York Ranger Andy Bathgate hit Plante in the face early in a Rangers-Canadiens contest. The puck opened a wound in his face that required seven stitches to close. Suffering that injury helped Plante make up his mind. When he returned to the ice after getting stitched up, he was wearing his face mask. It was the first time an NHL goalie had ever worn a mask in a regulation game. And it started a safety trend that has now become an acceptable part of modern hockey.

HERE ROVER

A modern hockey team is made up of six players: a center, two wingers or forwards, two defensemen, and a goalie. However, back in the early days of organized hockey, teams played with *seven* players on a side. The seventh player was called a "rover," and he went anywhere and everywhere, roaming around the outdoor rinks that most teams played on in those days. In 1910 the National Hockey Association (the forerunner of the NHL) became the first league to require its teams to skate with only six players on a side. The NHL has used six-player teams since its birth in 1917.

FROM BOOTH TO BENCH

In 1981 Mike Nykoluk was working as a radio color commentator for the Toronto Maple Leafs. A former NHL player, Nykoluk had been an assistant coach with the Philadelphia Flyers and the New York Rangers before deciding on a career as a radio announcer. Nykoluk liked talking about hockey, but apparently he liked coaching it even more. When Coach Joe Crozier of the Toronto Maple Leafs was released in January 1981, Nykoluk made another quick career move. He was named the Maple Leaf's head coach and went right from the Toronto broadcast booth to the Maple Leafs' bench!

DON'T SQUID ME

Bill Chadwick officiated a lot of NHL games as both a linesman and a referee during his long career (over 750 regular season NHL games and over 100 Stanley Cup playoff games). Like many referees, Chadwick couldn't always make everyone happy. Sometimes his calls (or the lack of a call) infuriated fans in the arena. Occasionally fans would get so made at him that they'd throw something at him.

Once, while Chadwick was refereeing a playoff game in Detroit in 1952, a fan didn't like his call and hurled something strange at him from the stands. Luckily Chadwick saw the object coming and ducked. When it landed on the ice, Chadwick saw that an angry fan had thrown a small squid at him!

ATTENTION

Many National Hockey League teams like to hear rock music in their dressing rooms before games. The players say that the music helps them to relax. Tom McVie, who coached the Washington Capitals in the mid-1970's, also liked having music in his team's locker room before games, but insisted on a certain kind of music. Instead of rock, McVie insisted his team listen to military marching bands. Tom McVie was convinced that listening to military marches helped inspire his team!

HO! HO! HO! HOCKEY!

In 1949 the New York Rangers prepared for their Christmas night game against the Toronto Maple Leafs in a truly festive way. The Rangers' center, Phil Watson, dressed up in a Santa Claus suit and skated through the team's pregame workout dressed as jolly old St. Nick. While attired in his red suit, Watson shot the puck, passed it, and even threw body checks while sports columnists, photographers, and reporters witnessed the wacky holiday publicity stunt. By the way, Watson changed into his regular uniform for the game and helped the Rangers beat Toronto 3–1 in their Christmas meeting. Then again, how could the Rangers lose with Santa on their side?

THE KICK IS GOOD!

New York Islander Bob Nystrom scored the 200th goal of his NHL career on February 16, 1982, in a game against the Pittsburgh Penguins. The goal was a milestone in Nystrom's career, but it wasn't exactly a classic shot. With Nystrom camped out in front of the Pittsburgh net, the Islanders' Tomas Jonsson fired a shot. The puck tipped off Bob Nystrom's stick and then accidentally bounced off his leg and skidded into the net for a goal. It wasn't pretty, but it counted for goal number 200!

ALMOST GOLDEN TWICE

H erb Brooks was the coach of the United States hockey team that won the gold medal at the 1980 Winter Olympics. The win was a great accomplishment for Brooks and his team but it wasn't the first time he had a close encounter with Olympic ice hockey gold. In 1960 Brooks was a member of the University of Minnesota's hockey team, and he tried out for the Olympic squad. Brooks was the last player cut from the 1960 U.S. ice hockey team, which went on to win a gold medal. So even though he missed out on an Olympic gold medal in 1960, he returned 20 years later to take his place in the Olympic record books.

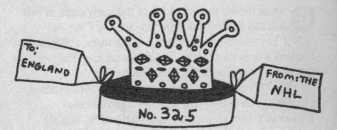

QUEEN'S PRIZE

I n 1952, the record for most career goals scored in the NHL stood at 324. In October 1952 Maurice Richard of the Montreal Canadiens tied that record. He then went on to break the record by scoring two goals in a game played on November 9, 1952. Richard kept the pucks that he fired into the nets for his 324th and his 326th goals as mementos. What happened to the 325th puck? It was forwarded by Canadian officials to Her Royal Highness Queen Elizabeth II of England as a souvenir.

A BIG PAYDAY

One of the hottest rivalries in the early days of pro hockey in Canada was between the Ottawa Silver Seven and the Renfrew Millionaires. Whenever the two teams met it was like a war on ice. Players on the two teams just did not like each other.

Fred "Cyclone" Taylor, a star for the Millionaires, once bragged that he could score against Percy LeSueur, Ottawa's outstanding goaltender, skating backwards. No one in Ottawa appreciated Taylor's boast. The next time the Renfrew team visited Ottawa, Taylor was pelted with rotten fruit thrown by the Ottawa fans every time he stepped onto the ice.

The rotten-fruit incident increased the bad blood between the Millionaires and the Silver Seven. Finally Ambrose O'Brien, the owner of the Millionaires, decided to get in on the feud. Before his team played Ottawa again, he offered his players a bounty on goals scored. O'Brien promised he would pay $100 for each and every goal scored by his team. The money was to be divided up equally among all of his players. In those days, $100 was a lot of cash.

When the two teams met again in 1910, all the Renfrew players could think about was the bounty their owner had posted. To make things even more interesting, O'Brien offered an additional $50 per goal to be paid to any player who scored a goal. The Millionaires were so worked up that they couldn't wait to get on the ice. When the game started they fired shot after shot at the Ottawa net. Goaltender Percy LeSueur was bombarded. The Millionaires ended up scoring 17 goals against the Silver Seven and recorded a 17–2 victory, which cost their owner an additional $2,550 in pay.

The lopsided win was embarrassing enough for Ottawa, but goaltender Percy LeSueur suffered even greater embarrassment. During the contest Fred "Cyclone" Taylor took a pass from teammate Newsy Lalonde. Taylor turned completely around and skated in backwards against LeSueur. Taylor then whipped the puck into the net for a Renfrew goal, finally making good on the boast that had so enraged Ottawa fans.

CUP CAPER

The Stanley Cup was enshrined in the Hockey Hall of Fame in 1963 for safekeeping. However, the Hall of Fame proved to be less than secure, because the Cup was stolen in 1970. A Toronto detective named Wallace Harkness was hired to find the missing Cup. Harkness hunted for the Cup for three weeks, and he was apparently closing in on the thieves. Something must have worried them, however, because the Cup was found lying on Wallace Harkness' driveway on Christmas night, 1970. No one was sure how it got there, but everyone involved in hockey was relieved to see it returned.

MONTREAL BOUND

The Stanley Cup has moved from city to city in North America as various teams have won the championship finals over the years. But in almost 100 years of Stanley Cup play, the trophy itself has spent more time in Montreal than in any other city. Through the years the Cup has been won by six different Montreal teams. The NHL's Montreal Canadiens have won the Stanley Cup 23 different times (as of 1992). The first team in Montreal to take the trophy was the Montreal AAA, which won the Cup three times. The other Montreal-based teams to win Lord Stanley's Cup are the Montreal Victorias (four times), the Montreal Wanderers (also four times), and the Montreal Shamrocks and the Montreal Maroons (twice each). In all the Stanley Cup has been housed in Montreal 38 times from 1898 to 1991.

FAST MAN WITH A STICK

Bobby Hull, who is best known as a player for the Chicago Black Hawks, really knew how to zip pucks past opposing goalies. It's no wonder that Hull scored over 1,000 goals in the National Hockey League and the World Hockey Association. His powerful slap shot was once timed at 118.3 miles per hour!

HAT TRICK!

Scoring three goals in one NHL contest is no easy task. But on March 23, 1952, Bill Mosienko of the Chicago Black Hawks apparently found that scoring three goals in a single game wasn't too difficult after all. In fact, Mosienko barely had time to raise a sweat when he rocketed three pucks past opposing goalie Lorne Anderson of the New York Rangers. With a little help from teammate Gus Bodnar, Mosienko scored the three quickest goals by a single player in NHL history. Mosienko, Chicago's captain, flipped three pucks in a row into the Ranger net in a mere 21 seconds! Gus Bodnar assisted on all three Mosienko goals, which came in the third period of play. It was one of the greatest achievements ever in the history of the NHL.

GET TO THE POINT

There's no doubt that Wayne Gretzky is one of the greatest scoring machines to ever put on a pair of skates. However, a lesser-known scorer named Darryl Sittler accomplished something Gretzky has yet to equal. Darryl Sittler of the Toronto Maple Leafs scored 10 points (6 goals and 4 assists) in a single NHL game against the Boston Bruins on February 7, 1976. As yet, none of the NHL's brightest stars has ever been able to equal Sittler's one-game scoring feat.

NAME GAME?

Hockey is a tough sport. Any team that plays for the Stanley Cup should look, play, and sound *tough*. Well, that wasn't the case in 1916 when the Montreal Canadiens took on the champions of the Pacific Coast Hockey Association for the Stanley Cup. The nickname of the PCHA champion team was the Portland Rosebuds!

TRAVELING MAN

Bill Stewart liked to change jobs. Before he took over as the rookie coach of the NHL's Chicago Black Hawks in 1937–38, he worked as an umpire in baseball's National League and then as a referee in the NHL! Although Stewart's coaching career didn't last long, he led Chicago to a Stanley Cup victory in his very first year as an NHL coach.

MERRY CHRISTMAS

On the early days of the NHL, the New York Rangers used to play on Christmas night. The game was a Ranger tradition, and the team usually had great success playing every December 25th. In fact, from 1933 to 1946 the Rangers had won 10 games, tied 1, and lost only 2 games. But in 1946 the prospect of a Ranger Christmas victory seemed highly improbable. The Rangers' opponent that year was the defending Stanley Cup champion Montreal Canadiens. During the same season that Montreal had won the Cup, the Rangers had finished dead last in their division. The Christmas 1946 game promised to be a terrible mismatch. But somehow the spirit of Christmas prevailed. The Rangers shut out the stunned defending champions by the score of 2–0. Amazingly, the Rangers' Christmas win spree continued for three more years. On Christmas night 1947 the Rangers beat the heavily favored Detroit Red Wings 2–0. The following year, the Rangers beat the Canadiens again on Christmas by the identical 2–0 score. And on Christmas 1949 the wrecking crew from New York defeated the Toronto Maple Leafs 3–1. Christmas sure was fun for the Rangers in those days!

BROTHER AGAINST BROTHER

On October 7, 1990, the Washington Capitals took on the Detroit Red Wings in Landover, Maryland. But this matchup wasn't an ordinary contest. The game pitted brother against brother as Terry Murray, the coach of the Washington Capitals, faced off against his older brother Bryan Murray, the coach of the Detroit Red Wings. A brother-versus-brother contest is a rare occurrence in the NHL. In this matchup, younger brother Terry didn't show much respect for his elder as Washington went on to defeat Detroit by the score of 6–4.

LIGHTNING FAST SCORE

On February 11, 1975, Kim Miles of the University of Guelph (Ontario) picked up a fast goal at the start of his game against the University of Western Ontario. Miles blasted the puck into the net a mere three seconds after the start of the contest!

TO FIGHT OR NOT TO FIGHT

F ighting on the ice has unfortunately been a part of professional hockey since the NHL began back in 1917. Players are expected to defend themselves and their teammates from opposing skaters who may try to get too physical. However, in February 1992, Shayne Corson of the Montreal Canadiens got into a bunch of trouble for fighting— and it wasn't on the ice!

It happened after a Montreal victory. Corson had gone out to unwind after the game, and was relaxing at a club when an argument started. Corson ended up getting into a fight, and the police were called. No charges were filed against him for his off-ice fighting, but he was suspended from the Canadiens team. It just goes to prove that fighting, even for hockey players, isn't a good way to settle one's differences.

NO GOALIE HOCKEY

It's not unusual for a pro coach to pull his goalie out of the game when time is running out and his team is losing. Yanking the goalie to put an extra attacker on the ice is usually a last desperate attempt to earn a tie or a win.

One night in 1950 during a Pacific Coast League contest Walter "Babe" Pratt, the coach of the New Westminster hockey team, decided that his goalie was expendable. New Westminster was losing to Vancouver by the score of 6–2 when Pratt decided to yank his goalie to put in another attacker. What was so strange about Pratt's decision was that there were still 14 minutes left to play in the game!

Everyone who saw the wacky maneuver was sure that Pratt had gone crazy. Nevertheless, he put an extra attacker on the ice and left his net defenseless. Strangely enough, his strategy worked! New Westminster went on to score four goals while holding Vancouver scoreless—even without the help of a goaltender. The game ended in a 6–6 tie. New Westminster avoided a loss by playing the final 14 minutes of its game without a goalie!

OUCH!

The Detroit Red Wings once scored 15 unanswered goals in a single game to beat the New York Rangers 15–0. The game took place on January 23, 1944.

I'LL TAKE THAT!

The Chicago Black Hawks won the Stanley Cup in 1960–61. Since they were the defending NHL champions, the Black Hawks had the Cup on display in a trophy case in the Chicago Arena when the Montreal Canadiens visited for a Stanley Cup playoff game during the 1961–62 season. The game went badly for Montreal, and it became obvious that the Canadiens would surely lose.

Watching in anguish from the stands was a die-hard Montreal fan. He couldn't stand watching Montreal lose. He believed the Stanley Cup trophy belonged in Montreal. He got out of his seat and went over to the trophy case that held the Stanley Cup. As play inside the arena continued, he pried open the trophy case and took out the huge Stanley Cup trophy. Carrying the trophy, he headed for the exit. He planned to personally take the trophy to Montreal. Unfortunately, ushers spotted him with the Cup and notified the police, who grabbed him before he could leave the arena. The Stanley Cup was rescued and the fan got off with a stiff reprimand from a Chicago judge. Ironically, neither Montreal nor Chicago won the title that year. The Stanley Cup ended up going to the Toronto Maple Leafs.

STICK TRICK

As you've already read, goalie Billy Smith of the New York Islanders was the first goalie in NHL history to get credit for scoring a goal. Billy's goal was a bit of a fluke, because he never actually shot the puck himself. But on December 8, 1987, goaltender Ron Hextall of the Philadelphia Flyers became the second goalie to score a goal in an NHL contest and *it* was no fluke.

The Flyers were playing the Boston Bruins in Philadelphia. Boston was losing 4–2 and needed to score, so the Bruins pulled their goalie out of the game in the final period of play. The puck was in the Flyers' end when Philadelphia goalie Ron Hextall pounced on it near his net. He whacked the puck high in the air with his stick, lifting it over players from both teams. The puck flew down the ice and slid into the empty net for a Philadelphia score! Hextall became the first NHL goalie to ever actually shoot a puck into the opposition's net.

LYING DOWN ON THE JOB

The Edmonton Oilers' Stan Weir scored in a strange way in 1980. In a game between the Oilers and the Los Angeles Kings, Weir was on the ice when he was knocked flat near the Los Angeles net by a Kings' defenseman.

Weir ended up lying flat on his back on the ice. While he was down, Edmonton's Risto Siltanen let a blazing 40-foot slap shot fly toward the Kings' net. The shot was off the mark just a bit, and was headed right for his teammate Stan Weir, who was sprawled on the ice and didn't see the puck coming. Luckily for Weir, the puck hit his stick and caromed toward the opponents' net, where it deflected past Kings' goaltender Mario Lessard for an Oilers' score! Since Weir was the last Edmonton player to touch the puck he received the goal. So Stan Weir ended up getting credit for a goal he never shot that bounced off his stick while he was sprawled on the ice.

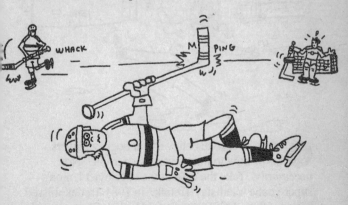

PHILLY PHOBIA

F or many years the NHL's Minnesota North Stars hated to travel to Philadelphia. It wasn't that the North Stars' players didn't like the city. It was just that every time the North Stars visited the Spectrum, the home arena of the NHL's Philadelphia Flyers, they seemed to lose confidence. They also lost a lot of games. From 1978 to 1988 the Minnesota North Stars did not win a single game against the Philadelphia Flyers in the Spectrum. But finally, on January 24, 1988, the North Stars ended their almost 10-year losing streak at the Spectrum by beating the Flyers on Philadelphia's home ice by the score of 5–3.

WHOOPS!

A lmost everyone believes that hockey players know how to maneuver on ice, right? Not necessarily. Take the case of the old Soviet Union's super goalie Vladislav Tretiak. In 1981 Tretiak missed playing in the USSR's National Hockey Championship because of a fluke injury. While stepping off a bus near Moscow, Tretiak slipped on a patch of ice in the street and fell and broke his leg!

THE MORNING AFTER

In hockey's early days there were no paid officials to call a game, so it was customary to use players as referees. In 1899 Fred Chittick, a goaltender for Ottawa, was called in to referee a game between teams from Montreal and Quebec. Unfortunately, Chittick had been out celebrating the night before and was in no condition to officiate that day. His calls were so bad that the Montreal players left the ice with 12 minutes left to play in the game and never returned to finish the contest. The game was never completed.

WATERED-DOWN VICTORY

The Kenora Thistles met the Montreal Wanderers in a game for the Stanley Cup in 1907. Before the game took place, the officials of both teams got into a big argument about which players were eligible to play in the contest. The meeting was held in a building near a lake. A Thistles official got so mad that he grabbed the Stanley Cup trophy and started out the door. He threatened to toss the trophy into the nearby lake if the matter couldn't be resolved. Luckily, it was. The Stanley Cup avoided a dunking, and Montreal beat Kenora in March 1907 to take the championship.

GOOD-BYE!

Goaltender Michel Dion of the Quebec Nordiques was having a tough time in goal when his team played the Boston Bruins in December 1980. While blocking shot after shot fired at him by a horde of Bruins players, Dion became convinced that his teammates weren't trying hard enough to help him and that the officiating in the game could use some improvement, too.

Dion got madder and madder as the game went on. Finally, when the officials allowed a disputed unassisted goal scored by the Bruins' Dick Redmond to count, Dion lost his temper. In the middle of the game he decided to stage a walkout. Dion zoomed out of his net and skated over to the Nordiques' bench, where he angrily dropped off his stick and glove. Then to everyone's astonishment he headed for the exit! Dion skated off the ice, left the arena, and didn't come back to finish the game. The Nordiques' coach, Michel Bergeron, couldn't believe his eyes, and neither could anyone else at the game. Quebec put in another goalie and lost the game 6–4, but Dion ended up the biggest loser. He was suspended from the team for his temperamental exit and was later traded.

SIBLING SHOOT-OUT

The Stastny brothers made scoring a family affair in an NHL game played on December 11, 1982. Peter, Marian, and Anton Stastny were all skating for the Quebec Nordiques when the team traveled to Pennsylvania to take on the Pittsburgh Penguins. In that game, which the Nordiques won 7–2, the Stastny brothers scored six of their team's seven goals! Peter scored three goals, Marian scored two, and Anton added one of his own. If that wasn't enough, the Stastnys also collected seven assists in that contest. Marian and Peter had three assists each and Anton tallied one assist. Now that's really keeping scoring in the family!

CALL THE REF

Referee J.A. Findlay caused an uproar in a Stanley Cup game in 1899 between two teams with the same name. That year the Winnipeg Victorias and the Montreal Victorias were involved in a tough contest. When Montreal's Bob McDougall hit Winnipeg's Tony Gingras with a stick, Gingras had to be carried off the ice. After checking on Gingras' condition, referee Findlay gave McDougall a two-minute penalty.

The Winnipeg players were furious — they believed the penalty should have been stiffer. So they went into their locker room and refused to continue the game! When referee Findlay couldn't convince them to come out, he angrily left the Montreal arena and went home. No one knew what to do. The game wasn't officially over.

A sleigh was sent to Findlay's house, and he was persuaded to return to the arena in the hope of resuming the game. But when Findlay returned, the Winnipeg players still refused to return to the ice. In fact, some of the players had already dressed and left the arena. This time Findlay awarded the victory to the Montreal Victorias and left the arena once and for all.

BAD LUCK

John Muckler was named the coach of the Buffalo Sabres after the 1991–92 season had begun. Muckler replaced former Buffalo coach Rick Dudley, who had been fired. Muckler's first game as the Sabres' new coach was very unlucky. His team lost to the Hartford Whalers 8–4 in a game that was played on Friday the 13th, 1991. What a day to start a head-coaching career!

NO FREE RIDES

In 1983 the Seattle Breakers of the Western Hockey League made an unusual deal with the Victoria Cougars of British Columbia. In one of the wildest minor-league hockey trades in history, Seattle swapped the rights to player Tom Martin to Victoria in exchange for a down payment on a bus owned by the Cougars!

GOALIE GOAL

Goaltender Fred Brophy of the Montreal Westmounts made hockey history in 1905 (before there was an NHL). Goalie Brophy's historic performance wasn't for keeping opposing players from scoring, however. He earned his way into the record books by actually scoring a goal himself. In a game against Quebec, Brophy took the puck out of his own end, skated down the ice, and fired a shot past opposing goalie Paddy Moran for a score! It was the first time in organized hockey that a goalie had ever scored a goal. Fred must have liked the feeling he got from scoring. The following year while tending goal for the Montreal AAA, Brophy scored another goal, this time against the Montreal Victorias.

SO LONG, FANS!

It's not easy to be an NHL official. Referee Red Storey found that out during the 1958–59 season while officiating a Stanley Cup semifinal playoff game between the Montreal Canadiens and the Chicago Black Hawks. During the game Albert "Junior" Langlois of Montreal appeared to trip the Black Hawks' star scorer, Bobby Hull. At least, that's what many Chicago fans believed. But Storey didn't see an infraction and made no penalty call.

The Chicago fans went berserk. Several rushed out of their seats, climbed over the boards, and ran out onto

the ice. They poured their drinks on the unfortunate referee's head and knocked him to the ice. The fans that remained in the stands threw everything they could find out onto the ice. The rink was soon covered with debris. The game had to be held up for 25 minutes while order was restored and the ice was cleaned.

Montreal went on to win the semifinal series against Chicago and eventually the Stanley Cup (defeating the Toronto Maple Leafs), but the incident was not forgotten, even after the series ended. When Storey heard that NHL president Clarence Campbell had reportedly criticized his call, he decided he'd had enough. Storey resigned his job as a pro hockey referee.

YOU AGAIN

In March 1975 Guy Lafleur of the Montreal Canadiens scored his 50th goal of the season in a game against the Kansas City Scouts (who became the Colorado Rockies and today are the New Jersey Devils). In the nets for the Scouts that night was goaltender Denis Herron. A year later Lafleur had another fine season. He scored his 50th goal in March 1976 against the Kansas City Scouts. Again the goalie who gave up that 50th goal was Denis Herron. Moving ahead to 1978–79, Guy Lafleur again tallied his 50th goal of the season in March. This time it came against the Pittsburgh Penguins. But in goal that night was a familiar face — none other than Denis Herron! Of course, Herron wasn't Lafleur's only victim. Guy scored at least 50 goals for 6 consecutive years between the 1974–75 and 1979–80 seasons.

SHAKE, PAL

King Clancy of the Toronto Maple Leafs never ran away from fights on the ice, but he did find novel ways to avoid them. Once during the 1930–31 season, Clancy was in Boston playing with the Maple Leafs against the Bruins. Playing for the Bruins that day was Eddie Shore, one of the toughest players ever to skate in the NHL. When Clancy knocked Shore into the boards during the game, Shore angrily dropped his gloves and prepared to slug it out with Clancy. Clancy immediately grabbed Shore's hand, shook it, and inquired about Shore's health. The stunt was so funny that even tough guy Shore had to laugh. There was no fight.

CUP COACH

When the New York Islanders won the Stanley
Cup four years in a row in 1980, 1981, 1982,
and 1983, Coach Al Arbour was thrilled. But all
those Stanley Cup victories were not a new
experience for Arbour. He was involved in winning
the Stanley Cup eight different times with four
different NHL teams. In addition to winning the Cup
as the coach of the Islanders, Arbour, as a player, was
a member of the Stanley Cup champion Detroit Red
Wings in 1954. When the Chicago Black Hawks won
the Stanley Cup in 1961, defenseman Al Arbour was
on the team. Arbour also played for the Toronto
Maple Leafs squad that won Stanley Cups in 1962
and 1964.

HI POP!

Gordie Howe played professional hockey until he
was 52 years old and was a great example to his
hockey-playing sons, Marty and Mark. In fact,
Gordie, Marty, and Mark played together for the
Houston Aeros of the old World Hockey Association,
and the three then skated on the same line for the
New England Whalers of the WHA, and then for that
team's successor, the Hartford Whalers of the NHL.

SORRY, PAL

Pro hockey players occasionally make a big goof by shooting the puck into their own net for a score against their own team. This usually happens when a team's goaltender has been pulled off the ice, and the net is left unguarded. Even though accidentally shooting the puck into your own unguarded net isn't acceptable, it is sometimes understandable.

Take the case of Lars Lindgren, a defenseman for the Vancouver Canucks in 1982. Lindgren accidentally scored a goal against his own team to give the Edmonton Oilers a 3–3 tie on November 20, 1982, but he did it the hard way. Vancouver was leading 3–2 with only nine seconds remaining in the contest when Lindgren picked up the puck deep in his own end. He wanted to pass the puck behind his own net, but what he wanted to do and what he ended up doing were two different things. Lars fired the puck in the direction of his own net. The puck hit the net's post and skidded behind Vancouver goaltender Ken Ellacott for a freak score. Lindgren not only scored against his own team, but beat his own goalie in the process. Edmonton's Mark Messier got official credit for the goal, because he was the last Edmonton player to touch the puck.

ICE CAPADES

I n 1980 the Colorado Rockies management wanted to improve the skating ability of the team's players. To do that, management hired an unusual coach. Dianne Holum, the coach of the U.S. Olympic speed-skating team, was hired by the Rockies to improve the skating of their players. Holum became a rarity in the NHL—a female coach!

GAME MEMENTO

I n the early days of hockey, pucks fired into the crowd were always tossed back into the rink. It wasn't until around 1930 that hockey fans began to keep pucks shot into the audience as souvenirs of the game!

TIRING SEASON

The 1971–72 NHL season called for a total of 78 regular-season games for each team. A 78-game season is long enough, but consider what happened to NHL star Ross Lonsberry that year. Lonsberry played in 82 regular-season games that year. Here's how it happened.

Lonsberry played his first 50 games that year with the Los Angeles Kings. On January 28, 1972, he was traded to the Philadelphia Flyers. At the time Lonsberry was traded, the Flyers had played only 46 games. Lonsberry then appeared in all 32 of Philadelphia's remaining games. So Lonsberry played 50 games for the Kings and 32 games for the Flyers in the 1971–72 season — four more regular-season games than most other players in the league participated in.

REVENGE

Upsala College of New Jersey took on Elmira College of New York in a Saturday night contest in January 1980. Upsala was outmanned and outgunned, and Elmira easily defeated them by the embarrassing score of 22–1. The same two teams were scheduled to meet again the next afternoon. Upsala's coach expected his team to do much better in that second match. And Upsala *did* improve in that second game. On Sunday afternoon Upsala lost by the score of only 19–1.

DOWN AND OUT

It's the goal-tender's job to keep the puck out of his net any way he can. Goalies sometimes sprawl, fall, and throw themselves on

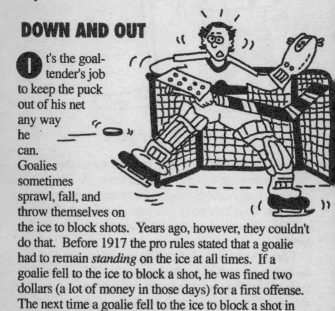

the ice to block shots. Years ago, however, they couldn't do that. Before 1917 the pro rules stated that a goalie had to remain *standing* on the ice at all times. If a goalie fell to the ice to block a shot, he was fined two dollars (a lot of money in those days) for a first offense. The next time a goalie fell to the ice to block a shot in the same game he was fined an additional three dollars and given a five-minute penalty. That silly rule was changed for the 1917–18 season, which made goaltending a little easier.

HELP!

The Chicago Black Hawks fought all the way to the Stanley Cup finals in the 1937–38 season. Unfortunately, Chicago's goalie, Mike Karakas, then broke a toe. When the Black Hawks met the Toronto Maple Leafs in the first game of the finals, Karakas was unable to play. His broken toe had become so swollen that he couldn't put his skate on. Since hockey teams in those days were allowed to have only one goalie on their rosters, Coach Bill Stewart had to scramble to find a substitute.

The only goalie available at the time was a minor-league goaltender named Alfie Moore, who happened to live in Toronto. Moore was hustled into the Chicago dressing room to suit up just minutes before game time. Amazingly, the last-minute minor-league sub played outstandingly and helped lead Chicago to a 3–1 opening-game win over his hometown team, the Maple Leafs.

Moore felt no allegiance to the Maple Leafs. In fact, after the game was over he skated past their bench and thumbed his nose at the Toronto players. Moore was later ruled ineligible by the NHL's president to play in any more Stanley Cup games for Chicago that season. However, he was on hand when Mike Karakas recovered enough to play goal again for Chicago and help the Black Hawks win the Stanley Cup trophy! The victory was all made possible by the contribution of a last-minute sub who played against his hometown team.

BACKSIDE SHOT

Stan Mikita was one of the Chicago Black Hawks' greatest players. Stan won the Hart Memorial Trophy as the NHL's Most Valuable Player twice (1966–67 and 1967–68) and the Lady Byng Trophy for Outstanding Sportsmanship twice (1966–67 and 1967–68). In addition to those awards Stan Mikita was known as a great scorer. He won the Art Ross Trophy as the NHL's leading scorer four times (1963–64, 1964–65, 1966–67, and 1967–68).

To score his *first* NHL goal, Mikita enjoyed some unusual and embarrassing luck. That goal came against the New York Rangers. Mikita was parked near the Rangers' net when teammate Bobby Hull uncorked a blazing slap shot. The shot was off the mark and accidentally hit Mikita right in the backside! The puck deflected off Stan's rear end and slid into the Rangers' net. Since Mikita was the last Black Hawk player to touch the puck, he got credit for the goal. That's the funny way Stan Mikita scored the first of his 541 NHL career regular-season goals.

FAMILY SPORT

t seemed like everywhere a hockey fan looked during the 1982 season there was an NHL player named Sutter. In all, *six* Sutter brothers played on NHL teams that year. Brothers Duane and Brent Sutter were members of the New York Islanders. Brian Sutter served as captain of the St. Louis Blues. Darryl Sutter was a member of the Chicago Black Hawks. And joining their brothers in the NHL were the twin Sutter brothers, Ron and Rick. Ron was a member of the Philadelphia Flyers, and Rick played for the Pittsburgh Penguins. Of course, if having six brothers in the league at the same time wasn't unusual enough for the Sutter family, they also made history in 1982 when Ron and Rick became the first set of twins to ever play in the NHL.

RIOT ACT

Maurice "Rocket" Richard of the Montreal Canadiens was involved in a fight with Hal Laycoe of the Boston Bruins on March 13, 1955. Because Richard hit Laycoe with his hockey stick, NHL president Clarence Campbell suspended Richard from playing for the Canadiens for the rest of the season, including the playoffs.

Canadiens fans were terribly angered by Campbell's decision. When Campbell showed up at a March 17, 1955, game at the Montreal Forum, fans pelted him with eggs and tomatoes. Things got so bad that a tear gas bomb was thrown on the ice by an angry fan. The game was quickly suspended and the Forum was evacuated. But even after the fans left the arena, they didn't cool down. The protest over Richard's suspension grew more violent. Store windows were broken and cars were damaged. It took police a long time to restore order. Nevertheless, Campbell did not change his mind, and Maurice "Rocket" Richard remained suspended for the rest of the season, despite the rioting of some angry Montreal fans.

BIG WINNER

Defenseman Ken Morrow was a member of the U.S. Olympic hockey team that won the gold medal at the 1980 Winter Olympics. After the Olympics, Morrow joined the New York Islanders and helped them beat the Philadelphia Flyers for the 1979–80 Stanley Cup championship. Once a winner, always a winner!

POWERLESS

The 1988 Stanley Cup finals matched the Boston Bruins against the Edmonton Oilers. Things looked dark for the Bruins, because the Oilers were leading the 7-game series 3 games to 0. But things got even darker before the fourth game was over.

With the score tied 3–3 late in the second period, the lights at Boston Garden suddenly went out. A huge power failure caused the arena to go black. Play had to be halted, and fans had to be evacuated for safety reasons. The lights failed at 9:32 P.M. and did not come back on until 10:07 P.M. After the lights came back on, officials decided to postpone the game because 95% of the fans were already outside the arena. As dark as it was for Boston that night, things got even worse in the series. Edmonton went on to win the game when it was resumed, and then the Stanley Cup, beating the Bruins four games to one in the series.

MEDAL MAN

I n 1980 the biggest upset of the Winter Olympic Games in Lake Placid, New York, was the United States hockey team's amazing gold-medal performance. The underdog U.S. team took first place in the hockey competition, defeating the powerful Soviet Union team along the way. One of the reasons the U.S. Olympic hockey squad had such great success that year was the outstanding play of its goalie, Jim Craig.

What most people don't remember is that the U.S. had *two* goalies on its 1980 hockey team. Craig's backup goaltender was Steve Janaszak. However, Janaszak never got to play in any of the Olympic contests, because Craig was so dazzling in the net. The U.S. hockey team went on to take first place in the competition, and Steve Janaszak, like the rest of his teammates, was awarded a gold medal. Strangely enough, however, Steve Janaszak won an Olympic gold medal in hockey without ever playing in an Olympic hockey game.

NO FAVORITISM

T he 1980–81 NHL season was a good one for the New York Islanders' Mike Bossy. Bossy equaled Maurice Richard's outstanding feat of scoring 50 goals in 50 games that year, and eventually went on to score a total of 68 goals for the season. Amazingly enough, Bossy tallied his 68 goals that year by scoring against 33 different NHL goalies!

SNOW JOB

The Buffalo Sabres took on the Los Angeles Kings on January 10, 1982, in a game that turned out to be a crowd pleaser, even though very few fans actually showed up. The game, which was played in Buffalo, attracted only 2,079 fans, the smallest crowd ever to show up for a hockey game at Buffalo's Memorial Auditorium. The contest attracted so few rooters because there was a raging blizzard going on outside. More than 12,000 ticket holders decided to wait out the storm at home. However, those patrons who did brave the elements were treated to a 6–4 Sabre win. They were given another treat as well. In appreciation, the Sabres' management provided the fans with free hot dogs and drinks after the second period.

BROTHERLY LOVE

Professional hockey has sometimes become a family affair. A number of famous hockey families have had brothers—even fathers and sons—play together in the NHL. However, a rare family get-together occurred when the New York Rangers played the Chicago Black Hawks on December 1, 1940. On the ice for the Rangers were brothers Luzz and Lynn Patrick and brothers Neil and Mac Colville. On the other side of the ice, skating for the Black Hawks, were brothers Bob and Bill Carse and brothers Max and Doug Bentley! It's not too often that two sets of brothers have played against two sets of brothers in an NHL contest.

FAMILY TRADITION

When Craig Patrick was named the head coach of the New York Rangers in 1980, he was following a great family tradition. Craig's grandfather was Lester Patrick, who coached the Rangers in 1926 and served as the team's coach or general manager until 1945. Craig's dad, Lynn Patrick, played forward for the Rangers from 1934 to 1946 and coached the team from 1948 to 1950. And the list doesn't stop there. Craig's uncle, Murray "Muzz" Patrick, was a defenseman for the Rangers for five seasons starting in 1936–37, and he also coached the team from 1953 to 1955 and in the 1962–63 season. He also served as the team's general manager from 1955 to 1964.

FIGHT TO THE FINISH

When the Colorado Rockies took on the Boston Bruins in January 1981, the game was a fight to the finish. In fact, the game was one big fight. There was a total of *60* penalties called in the contest, which was eventually won by the Rockies 4–1. By the time the game concluded, Boston had had so many players thrown out of the contest that only six Bruins remained. And those six Boston players didn't even have a coach to guide them. He had been chucked out of the game, too!

WRONG WAY LABINE

S coring a goal usually makes an NHL hockey player happy. But Leo Labine of the Detroit Red Wings wasn't very happy about a goal he scored in a game against the Montreal Canadiens.

There were only seconds to go in the final period, and Montreal was beating the Red Wings 1–0. The Canadiens had someone in the penalty box, and play was stopped for a faceoff in the Montreal end of the ice. To give his team a greater chance of scoring, the Detroit coach took his goalie out of the game and put in another attacker. It gave the Red Wings a big advantage but also left their net unguarded.

The players lined up for the faceoff. Labine took the faceoff for Detroit and won it. As quick as a wink he tried to pass the puck back to a teammate. Unfortunately his pass missed everyone and headed right for the unmanned Detroit net. As you probably guessed, the puck went into the net, and Labine scored a goal for Montreal against his own team. What made matters even worse, since no Canadiens player had ever touched the puck, Labine was credited for scoring the goal against Detroit, his own team!

SNOOZE ALARM

Getting into the Hockey Hall of Fame is exciting news. In 1982 Rod Gilbert, formerly of the New York Rangers, was an unexpected choice for the prestigious honor. Gilbert, who scored 406 goals and 615 assists for 1,021 points in 1,065 games from 1960 to 1978, did not expect to be elected. In fact, when Tim Moriarty of the Hall of Fame selection committee phoned the Gilberts' house, Rod didn't answer the phone. The news was conveyed to Gilbert's wife, Judy, who had to go fetch her husband. Since he wasn't expecting the honor, Gilbert was taking a nap and was sound asleep at the time.

ROAD HOGS

Most professional hockey teams like to skate on their home ice in front of a hometown crowd. Skating in one's home arena seems to give many teams a winning advantage. However, the Montreal Canadiens like to win at home *and* on the road. In fact, in 1982 the Canadiens became the first NHL team to ever win a total of 800 regular-season games on the road (from 1917 to 1982). Since then the Canadiens have continued to add to their record list of road victories. Some teams are just winners, no matter where they play.

GOAL-MOUTH CLOSED

I t is the job of a goaltender to keep the mouth of the net closed to opposing players. Goalie Alex Connell of the old Ottawa Senators certainly did that during the 1927–28 NHL season. Connell registered six consecutive shutout wins and held opponents scoreless for a record 461 minutes, 29 seconds of on-ice time.

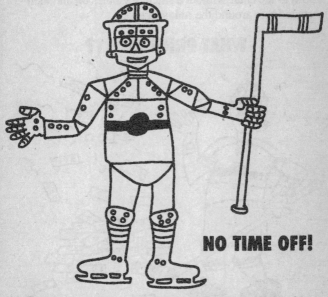

NO TIME OFF!

D oug Jarvis was an iron man of hockey during his playing days in the NHL. Jarvis, who played for the Montreal Canadiens, the Washington Capitals, and the Hartford Whalers, skated in a record 962 consecutive NHL contests from October 8, 1975, to October 10, 1987. In a game as physical as hockey where injuries abound, that feat is amazing!

BARE-CHAIR FEAT

At the 1992 Winter Olympics, players on the French national hockey team pulled a silly prank on one of their teammates at practice in a secluded arena. They tied poor Fabric Lhrenry to a chair and pushed him around the rink before he had a chance to put on his hockey pads. In fact, Lhrenry never had a chance to put *anything* on. His wacky friends secured him to the chair without a stitch of clothes on and then skated him around the rink as a joke.

WHAT PRICE GLORY?

Professional teams generally pay first-round draft choices a lot of money to sign a contract. In 1978 the Montreal Canadiens drafted Danny Geoffrion in the first round and signed him to a contract. Just two years later, however, Montreal let Geoffrion be claimed by the Quebec Nordiques for the low asking price of only $100. Talk about a drop in value!

LOSERS ARE WINNERS

The team that wins the Stanley Cup is supposed to be the best team in hockey. And the best team usually has the best record. But sometimes in the strange world of sports even losers can end up winners. Consider the case of the 1937–38 Chicago Black Hawks. The Black Hawks did not play exceptionally well that season, winning only 14 games while losing 25 and tying 9. Yet despite their mediocre record, the Black Hawks finished third in their division and qualified to play in the Stanley Cup playoffs. Amazingly, the Black Hawks got hot in the playoffs and went on to win the Stanley Cup, even though they lost more games than they won during the regular season!

The same strange thing happened again in 1948–49. The Toronto Maple Leafs finished the regular season with 22 wins, 25 losses, and 13 ties. The Maple Leafs also qualified for the playoffs and did extremely well. Toronto went on to capture the Stanley Cup even though they finished the regular season with a losing record.

BROKEN RECORD

Dickie Moore of the Montreal Canadiens won the NHL's scoring title in 1957–58 with an outstanding output of 84 points. Amazingly enough, Moore won the scoring race while playing the last five weeks of the regular season with a fractured wrist and a cast on his right arm!

HE DIDN'T WASTE ANY TIME

R ookie Gus Bodnar of the Toronto Maple Leafs didn't waste any time breaking into the scoring column in his first NHL contest. In a game against the New York Rangers on October 30, 1943, Bodnar scored his first NHL goal in his first NHL game just 15 seconds into the first period of play! What's equally amazing is that nine years later, Bodnar assisted on all three of the fastest three goals ever scored by one player (21 seconds, by Bill Mosienko; see story on page 47), thus giving him the record for the fastest three assists by one player, a record he still holds!

I'M REPLACING WHOM?

B ryan Murray liked to keep coaching in the family during his years as an NHL mentor. Bryan hired his younger brother, Terry, as his assistant coach while Bryan was head coach of the Washington Capitals. Unfortunately, in January 1990 the Capitals' management, upset with the team's eight-game losing streak, decided what the team needed was a coaching change. They dismissed Bryan Murray, who went on to become the head coach of the Detroit Red Wings. Who did the Capitals hire to replace departed coach Bryan Murray? You probably guessed already. They gave the head coaching job to Bryan's brother Terry.

WHAT'S IN A NAME?

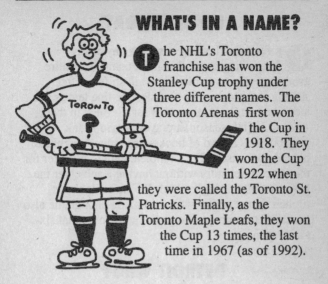

T he NHL's Toronto franchise has won the Stanley Cup trophy under three different names. The Toronto Arenas first won the Cup in 1918. They won the Cup in 1922 when they were called the Toronto St. Patricks. Finally, as the Toronto Maple Leafs, they won the Cup 13 times, the last time in 1967 (as of 1992).

BAD PENALTY

W hen a player receives a minor or a non-coincidental major penalty, his team has to play shorthanded for a specific amount of time or until the opposing team scores a goal. However, up until the 1956–57 NHL season, a player serving a minor penalty had to remain in the penalty box for the entire duration of his penalty, even if the opposing team scored a goal! It wasn't until the 1956–57 season that the NHL passed a rule allowing a player serving a minor penalty to return to the ice after the opposing team scores.

NO SUB TODAY

Professional hockey is such a physically demanding game that most teams use entire groups of players (called lines) in shifts. After skating and playing for a while, one line leaves the ice to rest while another subs for it. Back in the 1922–23 NHL season, a player named Frank Nighbor was a kind of hockey iron man. Nighbor played six consecutive, complete games at center for the Ottawa Senators without having a sub enter the game for him a single time! If Frank Nighbor's tireless feat at center wasn't amazing enough, he also managed to average one goal a game over that six-game span.

DETROIT WHO?

In 1926 the NHL team that played in Detroit was known as the Detroit Cougars. In 1930 they changed their name to the Detroit Falcons. Finally in 1932 the team changed its name to the Detroit Red Wings, the name by which they are known today.

FAST FIVE

The Pittsburgh Penguins once scored five goals in a single game in a mere 2 minutes, 7 seconds! It happened on November 22, 1972, in a game against the St. Louis Blues. The five fast goals were scored by Bryan Hextall, Jean Pronovost, Al McDonough, Ken Schinkel, and Ron Schock.

1000 poiNTs!

A RECORD YEAR

The year 1981 was a big year for three NHL stars. That year Marcel Dionne of the Los Angeles Kings, Guy Lafleur of the Montreal Canadiens, and Bobby Clarke of the Philadelphia Flyers all scored their 1,000th career NHL point!

MARSHALL LAW

When the Colorado Rockies played the Minnesota North Stars on November 30, 1981, the Rockies' players may have had some difficulty remembering just who their coach was. When the day began, Colorado's head coach was Bert Marshall. But before the game took place that evening, Bert Marshall was fired and replaced by new head coach Marshall Johnson. Luckily, the change didn't upset the Rockies too much. They managed to squeeze out a 2–2 tie against Minnesota.

WEIGHTY PROBLEMS

During the 1949–50 NHL season, weight was a big concern for Conn Smythe, the owner and coach of the Toronto Maple Leafs. First Smythe benched his starting goalie, Turk Broda, because he thought Turk was about seven pounds overweight. Smythe thought the extra weight slowed down Broda's reactions in net. He said that Broda wouldn't start again until he lost weight, and he put him on a diet to reduce. In the meantime, Smythe brought up goalie Gil Mayer from a minor-league team. Unfortunately, Smythe thought Mayer was too *slender* and put him on a program to gain weight!

While one Toronto goalie was dieting to lose weight and another was trying to gain weight, Smythe made a trade with the Cleveland Barons (no longer in the NHL) for a lanky goalie named Al Rollins. Smythe believed that Rollins was just the right weight to play well in goal. So Rollins played while Broda and Mayer stuck to their diets to earn a place on the team. Finally, Broda shed seven pounds and returned to share goaltending duties with Rollins. Unfortunately, Mayer never gained enough pounds to please the weight-conscious Conn Smythe and never earned a starting place on the Toronto team.

LETTER PERFECT

It looked like the Stanley Cup playoffs would be a short series in 1942. The Detroit Red Wings had won the first three games of the best-of-seven series against the Toronto Maple Leafs and the Red Wings were confident of victory. Almost everyone dismissed the Maple Leafs' chances of taking Lord Stanley's Cup. No other NHL team had ever come back to win four straight games and the Cup.

But Toronto coach Hap Day had a secret weapon up his sleeve. He had a letter written to the Toronto team from a 14-year-old girl who was a Toronto fan. She wrote that she was completely confident the Maple Leafs would win and that she was praying for their success. After Day read the letter to his players before game four of the series, Sweeny Schriner, a Maple Leafs player, assured Day that he and his teammates would win the Cup for the little girl. And Sweeny Schriner wasn't kidding.

Inspired by the letter, the Maple Leafs went on to beat the Red Wings in four straight games to take the Stanley Cup home to Toronto. It was the first time that a team had ever rallied to win the Stanley Cup after losing the first three games of the series. It was a miracle comeback by the Toronto Maple Leafs in 1942, and it was all inspired by a letter written from a 14-year-old fan to her favorite team.

LORD STANLEY'S CUP

Lord Stanley was England's Governor-General of Canada in 1892 when he decided to create a challenge-cup competition in ice hockey to determine a national champion of the sport he loved.

Lord Stanley arranged for a gold-lined silver cup to be made in England that would be presented to the team that was crowned the national champ. The Cup, which originally cost $48.67 (Canadian) to create, was ready to be presented in 1893, but a complication arose. Hockey teams from Ottawa and Toronto were supposed to play for the Cup, but Ottawa refused to travel to Toronto for any hockey contests, so no games were played.

The first actual games for the Stanley Cup took place on March 22, 1894, with Montreal AAA beating Ottawa in the finals for the title. Ironically, by the time the games were played, Lord Stanley had been recalled to England. The man who paid for the Stanley Cup and helped create the Stanley Cup playoffs never had a chance to see a single Stanley Cup game.

THAT'LL TEACH YOU!

Mel Hill was small for an NHL hockey player, even in 1938–39 when he tried to make the New York Rangers team. When the Rangers decided to release Hill, the Boston Bruins signed him to a contract. Hill didn't exactly light up the scoreboard with his goal-scoring ability. In fact, he scored only 10 regular-season goals that year for Boston. However, the Bruins managed to make it to the Stanley Cup finals that season, and Mel Hill was a part of the team. Playing in the Stanley Cup finals in 1938–39 gave him great satisfaction, because the Bruins' opponents in the finals were the New York Rangers.

The first game between the Rangers and the Bruins was tied at the end of regulation play. That meant the contest had to be decided by sudden-death overtime. The first team to score a goal would win. The Bruins notched the goal to beat the Rangers in overtime in game one of the Stanley Cup finals. Who scored that winning goal for Boston? None other than the Ranger castoff Mel Hill.

Several games later the Rangers and Bruins again ended up tied and had to play a sudden-death overtime period. Again the Bruins won the game in sudden death—on a goal scored by Mel Hill.

Finally, in the seventh and deciding game of the 1938–39 Stanley Cup finals, the two teams finished tied again. And who do you think scored the winning goal for Boston in sudden-death overtime to defeat the Rangers and help Boston take the Stanley Cup? A little guy named Mel Hill!

DON'T LOOK

In 1979 fans went to Maple Leaf Gardens in Toronto to watch the Toronto Maple Leafs take on the St. Louis Blues. However, what the fans saw before the contest was a bit strange, to say the least. A 25-year-old male fan leaped out of the stands and skated around the rink before anyone could stop him. The problem was that the fan had ice skates on and nothing else! The uninvited guest skater sped around the rink for about 30 seconds before police finally grabbed him and put an abrupt end to his shocking skating exhibition.

OVERCROWDED

Montreal has always been a great hockey town, but how many hockey teams can one city support? In 1910 there were two major hockey leagues in operation, the Eastern Canadian Hockey Association and the National Hockey Association. The ECHA had three teams based in Montreal—the "Shamrocks," the "Nationals," and "the All-Montreal" team. The NHA had two of its teams based in Montreal. They were the "Wanderers" and the "Canadiens." In all there were *five* major Montreal hockey teams in operation at the same time. Finally, to cut down on inter-league competition, the ECHA merged into the NHA. The Montreal member teams were cut down to three squads, the Wanderers, the Shamrocks, and the Canadiens. Today, only the Canadiens are members of the NHL.

FOOT FEAT

L eft wing Barry Tabobondung got stuck in an awkward position at the 1981 NHL draft, which was held at the Montreal Forum. Tabobondung was sitting in the audience with fans and other spectators when the Philadelphia Flyers announced that he was their third-round draft pick. The crowd cheered wildly as Barry stood up. He then tried to climb over some empty folding seats to meet with officials from the Flyers. Unfortunately for Tabobondung, he got his foot stuck in one of the seats. No matter how hard he tried, he could not get it out. People tried to help him free his foot, but no one could get the job done. Finally a carpenter had to be called to saw the chair apart.

PUCK BARRAGE

N ew York Ranger goalie Lorne Worsley once stopped an incredible 269 shots from opposing players in the span of only six games! It happened during the 1962–63 NHL season.

GOAL MINER!

I n 1905 a hockey team from Dawson City in the Yukon Territory, Canada, traveled 4,400 miles by dog sled, ship, and train to take on the Ottawa Silver Seven in a series for the Stanley Cup, which Ottawa had won the previous year. Unfortunately, the Dawson City Klondikers would have been better off if they had stayed home. Ottawa beat the Klondikers 9–2 in the first game of the series and demolished them 23–2 in the second and deciding game.

In that second Silver Seven victory, Ottawa's Frank McGee scored an unbelievable *14 goals* to set a pre-NHL record (the NHL wasn't formed until 1917). What's even more fantastic is that McGee tallied 8 of his 14 goals in a span of only 8 minutes, 20 seconds. He scored 3 other goals in a mere 90 seconds. Most amazing of all, McGee was partially blind and could see out of only one eye! Frank McGee was later named to the Hockey Hall of Fame.

TOUGH TIMES

T he Spokane (Washington) Flyers of the Western Hockey League got into financial trouble in 1981. Things got so bad that the team couldn't even afford to travel to Victoria, British Columbia, to play a scheduled game. So Spokane didn't bother to show up for the contest. As a result of missing that game, the league president suspended Spokane indefinitely from the league. Money may not make the world go round, but it sure is necessary when it comes to making road games.

A GOOD THING

Goaltender Terry Sawchuk of the Detroit Red Wings led the NHL in shutouts in 1951–52 by holding opposing teams scoreless in 12 of 70 games that season. The following year Sawchuk didn't lead the league in shutouts (Montreal's Gerry McNeil and Toronto's Harry Lumley shared the lead in 1952–53 with 10 shutouts each), but he regained the shutout title in both 1953–54 and 1954–55. Oddly enough, when Sawchuk again led the league in shutouts in 1953–54 and 1954–55, he repeated his identical record of 1951–52. Sawchuk had 12 shutouts in 70 games in 1953–54 and 12 shutouts in 70 games in 1954–55. So in three out of four years, Detroit's Terry Sawchuk led the NHL with 12 shutouts in each season.

INDEX